L. U. Reavis

A Lecture on What Shall we do to be Saved?

L. U. Reavis

A Lecture on What Shall we do to be Saved?

ISBN/EAN: 9783337313203

Printed in Europe, USA, Canada, Australia, Japan

Cover: Foto ©Lupo / pixelio.de

More available books at **www.hansebooks.com**

TO RUTHERFORD B. HAYES.

THE MAN,

WHOSE CONDUCT THROUGH LIFE HAS WON FOR HIM HONORS, SUCH
ONLY AS DUTY IN PRIVATE AND PUBLIC PLACE
AWARD TO THE FAITHFUL;

THE CITIZEN,

WHOSE RARE VIRTUES HAVE GIVEN STRENGTH ALIKE TO THE INDIVIDUAL
AND THE COMMUNITY, ATTESTING A NOBLE MANHOOD
WORTHY OF EXAMPLE AND IMITATION;

THE CHIEF MAGISTRATE,

WHO, WALKING WHERE WASHINGTON AND LINCOLN LEAD THE WAY, HOLDS
SECURELY THE TRUST OF A NATION COMMITTED TO HIM, AND
IN WHOSE KEEPING, FOR A TIME, IS REPOSED THE
PROSPERITY OF THE PEOPLE AND THE
HONOR AND SACRED TRUSTS
OF THE REPUBLIC,

THESE PAGES,

THE PRESENTATION OF AN EARNEST WORD IN BEHALF OF AMERICAN
INTERESTS, ARE RESPECTFULLY INSCRIBED BY

THE AUTHOR.

TO THE READER.

I have endeavored, in the following lecture, to present a line of discussion which I believe to be valuable to the American people in aiding to direct their efforts to maintain law and order, and to build up the American nation and promote the civilization of the country.

My faith in reference to the political affairs of the country is founded upon the views and principles of Alexander Hamilton. And in so far as his teachings can be wrought into the constitution of this government, according to the most enlightened and best judgment of our living statesmen, so far do I believe it to be the bounden duty of those charged with making and administering the laws to speedily act.

If I err in my estimation of Mr. Hamilton, I err with many illustrious men of America. Said Mr. Benton in writing of Hamilton :

He was the man most eminently and variously endowed of all the eminent men of his day—at once soldier and statesman, with a head to conceive and a hand to execute ; a writer, an orator, a jurist ; an organizing mind, able to grasp the greatest system ; an administrative, to execute the smallest details ; wholly turned to the practical business of life, and with a capacity for application and production which teemed with gigantic labors, each worthy to be the sole product of a single master intellect, but lavished in litters from the ever-teeming fecundity of his prolific genius. Hard his fate, when, withdrawing from public life at the age of thirty-four, he felt himself constrained to appeal to posterity for that justice which contemporaries withheld from him. And the appeal was not in vain ; statues rise to his memory, history embalms his name, posterity will do justice to the man who at the age of twenty was " the principal and most confidential aid of Washington," who retained the love and confidence of the father of his country to the last ; and to whom honorable opponents, while opposing his systems of policy, accorded honor, and patriotism, and social affection, and transcendent abilities.

Apart from the duty of perfecting the American system of government, the vast territorial extent of our country, the inexhaustible resources, the boundless facilities for commercial transportation and the intercommunication of the people, all bespeak a rapid and imperial growth of wealth, invention and population, which will constantly interweave the relations of government and civilization and increase the responsibility of the individual to the community and the duty of the government to the people. All these considerations require a wise and patriotic enactment and administration of the laws essential to the growth and progress and destiny of the country.

My purpose has been, in the production of these pages, to express in an earnest way a few thoughts touching the American system of government and the interests of the people, under the Constitution, with a view, if possible, to contribute some good to the general discussion, by adding, as I believe, some thoughts worthy of recognition. If I have accomplished this end, even in the smallest way, I shall deem my labor not in vain. For, be my labors many or few, my work much or little, I have an abiding faith in an imperial destiny of the Saxon blood on this continent and this hemisphere, and under the American Constitution. I see with the eyes of my soul that destiny slowly but surely growing out of the genius, the industry and the mental activity of the people. And to that destiny let all men be committed.

L. U. REAVIS.

St. Louis, Mo., *November* 1, 1877.

EXPLANATORY WORDS.

What shall we do to be saved?

There is no Liberty, but the Liberty of Law.

License, without the authority of Law, leads to Anarchy.

Full work and full pay is the Law for him who owns and him who earns.

" For if they do these things in a green tree, what shall be done in the dry?"

" Our national birth was the beginning of a new history, the formation and progress of an untried political system, which separates us from the past and connects us with the future only; and so far as regards the natural rights of man, in moral, political and national life, we may confidently assume that our country is destined to be the great nation of futurity."

I desire to speak to you of human powers and of human sufferings; of the powers and the sufferings, not of the selected Few to whom Fortune has assigned property and station, and along with these, voice and influence in the world's councils; but of the Children of Labor, of the millions who say little and do much, by whom the world is fed and clothed, by whom cities are built and forests subdued, and deserts reclaimed. I desire to speak of those whose strong arms ceaselessly tugging at the oar, have impelled through all time the bark of life; and briefly to ask of the Past how it has treated them; of the Present, what is their actual condition; of the Future, what may be their coming fate?—*Robert Dale Owen.*

It is a remarkable fact that the several successive streams of westward migration of the white Aryan race, from the primitive Paradise, in the neighborhood of the primeval cities of Sogd and Balkh, in High Asia, long separated in times of migration, and for the most part distinct in the European areas finally occupied by them, and which, in the course of its grand march of twenty thousand years or more, has created nearly the whole of the civilization, arts, sciences and literature of this globe, building seats of fixed habitation and great cities, successively, in the rich valleys of the Ganges, the Euphrates, the Nile, the rivers and isles of Greece, the Tiber and the Po, the Danube, the Rhine, the Elbe, and the Seine and Thames, wandering children of the same great family, are now, in these latter times, brought together again in their descendants and representatives, Semitic, Pelasgic, Celtic, Teutonic, and Sclavonic, here in the newly discovered common land of promise, and are commingled (especially in this great Valley of the Mississippi,) into one common brotherhood of race, language, law and liberty.—*Nathaniel Holmes.*

WHAT SHALL WE DO TO BE SAVED?

LADIES AND GENTLEMEN:

Man is the governing being upon the globe. He is the most perfect fruit on the tree of life. Through all time his aspiration has been to achieve freedom and happiness. This desire of his nature was decreed in the constitution of his being by Him who fixed the stars in the heavens, and ordered life to come forth on the planets and suns of space. This aspiration is therefore divine, and it constantly stimulates the race to a higher plane of social, political, intellectual and moral existence. It encourages men and women, in private and public life, to exercise all the faculties of each to obtain happiness in unfettered freedom. This stimulator of human action, this passion for aspiration, this ambition of man, has impressed itself on the life-deeds of the world's people, through all the evolutions of individual and public effort. We are enabled by the agency of history and discovery to trace through the long and weary centuries of the past, its operation through art and science, through the various forms of religion that have grown out of the human mind, and through all the governments of the world. Out of this element of the mind of man, grew communities, societies, cities, states and nations; they were, and are, the legitimate results of intellectual forces operating to attain freedom and happiness, individual or collectively, and, rightly directed by intellectual aid, this function of the mind will constantly impel man on to seek a wider range of freedom and happiness in the future. For the exercise of this function of the mind, legitimately interpreted, is nothing more than the natural growth of the human race, whether in individual, social or national life. As the individual has a growth, so has the race; and as the family has a growth, so has the nation. The foundation and government of the family has been the same in all ages, because the principles that govern the family have always been organic and not conventional. Not so with nations. Their principles and modes of life have always been conventional and not organic, and for this cause social and industrial revolutions have swept over the earth, and empires have been drenched in blood to secure the mastery of irreconcilable creeds and conventional usages of peoples living under the rule of different governments.

To attain organic conditions in national life, has been the political struggle of the human race. Up through all the forms of governmental association achieved by humanity—through savageism, barbarism, despotism, limited monarchies, empires and kingdoms to transitional republicanism—has the advanced body of all peoples struggled from age to age to attain organic liberty. Coming up from an infantile state of human growth, the form and condition of governments advanced with the intellectual and moral growth of mankind. In the order of advancement, the lower forms of government first appeared in Asia and Europe, and there they have had and do now hold exclusive sway on those continents. In the old world the thought of self-government has been little more than a dream of an enthusiast. Since history first began, centuries have rolled away, and nations have succeeded nations in the great struggles to eliminate a more perfect government for the people. The savage chieftain, the patriarch, the warrior and the king have each led their soldiers to battle, in defense of some real or imaginary right or supposed principle of government, unmindful of the fact that each struggle, that every defeat and every victory, was an unconscious effort of those who achieved it to attain a higher political life and a more advanced civilization. But in the long play of that unconscious drama, that has strewn Asia and Europe with the wrecks of centuries, only God knew the result—the end to be attained. The passions and propensities of men had ruled in Europe and Asia, and the thirst for vengeance had been satiated in savageism. Barbarism had fulfilled its mission. Tyrants and kings had already exhausted their ambition on the thrones of the world, and by the dawning light of future centuries mankind began to see afar off the people's advent. The world was already ripe for a new and more advanced form of government for the people. But nowhere in Europe or Asia could be found a land whereon to erect this new fabric of government about to be unfolded, and nowhere was a people to be found over which to build this new form of government, and into whose keeping it could be committed. But God alone had in charge the birth of this new child of the nations, soon to be born into existence—a revelation of a new and greater national life than had yet appeared upon the earth. In the councils of infinite wisdom He prepared the land on which this new nation was to be born, and sent out over the waters a greater than Noah, to discover the new land—

"The rich and wise Cathay
Columbus sought. faith-guided on his way."

THE BIRTH OF THE AMERICAN UNION.

The land was found—a continent of imperial grandeur, destined to be the home of an imperial Republic of States. God prepared a people to live in this new land. They sought its shores in due time, fleeing from persecution and tyranny, and in the fulness of time the new nation came forth revealed to the world, a shining fact; and well might the evening and the morning of the old and the new age form another day of creation, and the sun again stand still in the heavens to behold such a nation born into existence.

The organization of the American Nation was an achievement in national government far in advance of all previous efforts in the organization of political societies. It was the nearest approach to a correct political system that has ever been made by men. The wisdom of man and God seemed to combine in the creation of a continent and a nation perfectly compatible with the highest uses of both. For here is the great continent of the world, and here the great Republican nation of futurity. To consider this nation and the welfare of the people who live under the Constitution, is the purpose for which I stand before you. I am here to propound and consider a question of momentous concern to the American people. I am here to ask, "What shall we do to be saved?" A similar question was asked by a sinning, erring one near eighteen centuries ago. It was propounded to one of the founders of the Christian religion. I am not here to consider salvation for sinners, but for this nation. And before entering upon the consideration of the subject I wish it distinctly understood, that while I desire the well-being of all peoples, it is more important to save a nation than it is to save a sinner. Actuated by this conviction, I propose to consider some of the means of salvation essential to the existence of this nation and to the welfare of its people. But in so doing I do not wish to imply any undue alarm about the rapid approach of some social and political disaster of a national character, for I see none in the near future. I see no impending social crisis, no coming conflict, no immediate organic change in national life, that cannot be averted by the proper use of the means of salvation. But I do see an impending vital necessity for a higher growth of individual and national life—a growth commensurate with the necessities of a higher and more complex public life on this continent. I see many errors to correct, many reforms to make, many new questions to confront and solve—all means of salvation for this imperial Republic of States. In the discussion, however, I do not intend to indulge those of extreme temperaments, of calculating and cautious natures, nor the miser who pays taxes grudgingly, for these are constantly excited about every commercial, industrial, social and political incident that does not promise to bring to them a bountiful reward of luxury and wealth. Nor do I propose to take the side of the hypocrite, the fault-finder and the self-appointed judge of right and wrong. My purpose is to look beyond all incidental considerations touching individual, social and national life, and deal only with some of those things and conditions which now tend to disturb the organic structure of our social and political fabric, and, if possible, herald a better national life.

The vastness of our continental domain, and the extended rule of the Constitution over the diverse climates under which our people now and henceforth are to live ; the all-pervading growth of population, of commerce, of industry and government—all these constantly beget new and unsolved problems and conditions essential to the public life. To consider these things is the duty before us, and to consider them in a higher aspect shall be my endeavor.

In the field of public discussion it is believed that he who takes hold of a great truth, whether of adoption or of his own discovery, and proclaims it to the world and gives the earnest efforts of his life to its promotion and achievement, is the one most worthy the honors of true fame. It was for doing this, for devoting a life to the promotion and achievement of the principles of the Declaration of Independence, that, as Chas. Sumner said, won for Abraham Lincoln the honors of true fame.

It is my profound sentiment that America is the providential land of the world, and this conviction grows with increasing years. I do not say that this land and this nation is the especial work of some divinity of miraculous character ; but I do believe with Shakspeare that there is a divinity that shapes our ends, rough-hew them as we may ; and I believe with another, that through the years and the centuries, through things and atoms, through evil and good, a great and beneficent tendency irresistibly streams. Upon this I stand in conducting my discussion. I believe that all other governments of the earth have struggled through all time to produce the American Nation, and that on this continent are to be solved the great problems of the world.

THE AMERICAN SYSTEM OF GOVERNMENT, AND ITS MAINTENANCE.

Our fathers defined our government to be a Confederated Republic. We call it a Republic. It is strictly neither ; or in other words, the fabric or theory of our government may be defined either to be a Confederated

Republic or a Republic ; but the workings of the government are not far advanced in republicanism. We only have transitional republicanism, which consists in a declaration of principles without the practice. This nation is a child of a despotism, and a child always inherits some of the traits of the parents. We everywhere have resolutions declaring life, liberty and the pursuit of happiness to be inalienable in men, and we have enactments designed to secure these natural rights and conditions to every citizen : but such are the transitional conditions of the principles and practice of our people, under the laws, that nowhere under the flag is the citizen's life, liberty and happiness beyond the reach of peril. These are grave facts and command the attention of all people, but they are facts which belong to a condition of growth in the order of national development. The struggle of the race, in every mode of life, has always been an effort to rise from a lower to a higher plane, and it was impossible in the very nature of things for any part of the human race to skip a single link in the chain of national life, from savageism to organic liberty, which will succeed transitional republicanism on this continent.

It has been declared by the best writers on government that the most perfect form of government was that which approached nearest to nature, thus securing to man his natural rights. In the heat of the most memorable debate that ever took place in the United States Senate Mr. Webster exclaimed, "Would you re-enact the law of God?" Mr. Seward promptly replied, "You have no right to enact any other."

The founders of the American system of government, standing at the highest point of national advancement in the world's history, and standing upon the world's land of promise with all history before them, and looking to the establishment of an imperial Republic of States over a vast continent, and educated by the experience of all former governments, with a combined wisdom which seemed akin to divinity, adopted the principle of "equal and exact justice to all, exclusive privileges to none." They made the one mighty step in advance of all previous forms of government and erected a new nation on this new land, the principles of which more nearly approached the laws of God than ever before attained by man. That form of government was adapted to the conditions of the people destined to live upon this continent, as demonstrated by the topographical character of its wide domain. They created a constitution founded upon the natural rights of man, and thus gave birth to a new national life, destined to grow from transitional republicanism to organic liberty. Having inherited such a form of government, such a germ of national life, such a child of providence, with every promise of future growth in greatness and perfection, an over-mastering duty, a self-imposing obligation, demands of us its preservation and perpetuation.

A nation founded on human rights should be based on the will of the people, and if it is true that the will of the people must be founded upon intelligence for the purpose of giving inherent strength to the government, which I admit, the great question still follows, in reference to the obligation of the people to maintain and perpetuate the form of government organized by the first settlers upon the soil.

Is it not time for the American people to consider whether those now living under the Constitution have the right to voluntarily overturn the government established by our fathers, on the plea of the rights that inhere in the self-governed? I do not refer to the destruction of government by revolution, but by the voluntary action of the people. To be more explicit, I assume that though the people may possess all governmental power, in the name of representative government or natural rights, they have no right to overturn this or any other form of government, save by the right of revolution. Therefore I hold that this nation, though it be free only as God can create man, has the inherent right, superior to all men, to protect its own existence as the strong man has to protect his life. If this be true—and I challenge the world to disprove it—is it not full time to squarely meet a wide-spread conviction that demands a reconsideration or re-statement of the fundamental principles upon which free government stands? If it be true that a representative government is founded upon the consent of the people, does it follow that the consent of the people must constantly be reasserted in order to maintain the government? Would not such an admission be fatal to the maintenance of national life? In the very nature of things, if the public consent has to be constantly reaffirmed, we have no guarantee for the future of the nation. It is therefore high time that the American people abandon some of the loose notions about a government of the people. Even the use of the ballot does not imply a power in the hands of the people to overthrow the government. It does not imply the right to reaffirm self-government by the consent of the people. This nation is a legal compact : our fathers based its principles on the natural rights of man. At any rate, so far as human wisdom could determine, they made it a government of the people, declaring it to be founded upon certain inalienable rights belonging to men. Those who lived upon the territory over which the Constitution was first extended accepted its provisions and its rule as the supreme law of the new nation. Those living in different regions of country which the government of the thirteen original

States possessed, and the regions thereafter purchased, yielded to the supremacy of the Constitution and became integral parts of the Union and citizens under its provisions. They yielded to the supremacy of the fundamental law without reservation.

All who now live under the rule of the Constitution are bound to obey, to support and aid in maintaining the government and the liberties of the people. This government is not a mere rope of sand; it is a government of law, perpetual and enduring. Its ordinances were laid in the highest and divinest rights of men, and when the citizen as the individual accepted the Constitution as the shield of his rights, he entered into a legal compact for the maintenance of those rights, and neither one or more individuals has the right, under the plea of self-government, to reaffirm his obedience to the fundamental law. He has accepted the law for his rule of action, and he cannot abolish it. The dream of self-government without law is a phantasy of the mind. It is the highway-man's plea. It is the plea of the outlaw, for there is no liberty but the liberty of law. Let this be the axiom, the rock on which to hence-forth maintain the national fabric; and if it be true that there is no liberty but the liberty of law, we have secured the foundation of this and future nations upon the unchangeable principles of right with the power to repress wrong. When our fathers laid the foundation of this govern-ment upon the axiom that there was no liberty but the liberty of law, they gave the nation the right of self-preservation, and this right belongs as much to nations as it does to individuals; but the declaration of a right, or even the adherence to right conduct by one people, does not imply obedience to right by their successors. Men are prone to stray from the path of duty. Hence it was that Machiavelli said that, "accord-ing to the judgment of all authors who have written of civil government, and the examples of all history, it is necessary to whoever would estab-lish government, and prescribe laws for it, to presuppose all men natur-ally bad, and that they will show and exert that natural malignity as often as they have occasion to do it securely; for, though it may possibly be concealed for some time, it is for some secret reason, which want of precedent and experience renders invisible, but time discovers it after-wards." This doctrine of the great Italian statesman is not without a truth for its foundation. The experience of all mankind has demonstrated that, however wise men may be who found nations, and however pure and patriotic the people may be who assume new forms of government, there will arise in after times those who, actuated by some scheme of ambition, or passion for power and for gain, will seek to defy the law, and lead the people to deeds of violence and ruin. It is not the wisdom of the founders of governments, nor the correctness of the form of government, that make men good and obedient citizens. But the government that admits of the free and unrestrained development of all the faculties of the mind and the freedom of the individual, within the sphere of duty, is justly commendable to all mankind as being more nearly the true government. It is beyond human wisdom to prevent the birth and being of the bad as well as the good. It has, therefore, been necessary, when organizing a government based upon the natural rights of man, whereby to promote perfect freedom, to also enact laws to restrain the bad, and the creation of self-government has not been an exception to this rule. Hamilton, the master nation-builder known to the human race, foresaw at the time of the organization of the American Union, the possibility of bad men coming up in the future, whose vain endeavor would be to lead the people astray, and thus foreseeing, labored to put sufficient strength into the national fabric to enable the administrators of the law to contend against the aggressions of wrong-doers. Each succeeding decade in our national life has furnished additional evidence of the wisdom of Hamilton. He contended, as all reasonable men must contend, that to give strength to a nation would not necessarily take any liberties from the people ; that a government of the people, a representative government, could be made as strong as any other form of government without taking away any rights from the people.

If we assume as a fundamental axiom of government that there is no liberty but the liberty of law, it follows as a truth that the liberty of a people depends upon the strength of a government. Men are often led astray in their reasoning, and confound license with liberty. There is a wide difference in the meaning of the two terms. License is the liberty of wrong unrestricted by law. The liberty of law in a government of the people is for the protection of individual rights and the restraint of individual wrongs. License without the authority of law will soon lead to anarchy, while law to protect the good and restrain the bad will enable man to build for himself nations and cities, and create wealth and promote intelligence. Which will you choose? Shall we maintain a free nation on this continent, as God designed it should be, or shall we surrender it to lawless mobs? Those who have entered into the national compact have no more right, by banding together, to violate any part of the law than a highwayman has to take the life of his fellow-man. The law is as sacred to those who obey as life is to those who desire to live ; and he who comes forth to brave the law and imperil life in violation of rights, by the exercise of power that he does not rightly possess, must be regarded a criminal, and upon whom the penalty of the law ought to be executed. And if experience has recently taught us that anything is wanting in the fundamental law to give greater strength to our government, whereby to enable the officers of the law to restrain those who band together to trample down the rights and imperil life or the public welfare, let us rise to the dignity and necessity of the duty, and so change and amend the fundamental law as to give the strength required. It is the duty of the American people to maintain this government at all hazard ; and if it be true that national strength does not imperil the liberties of the people, any delay on the part of legislators to create the strength required will make them culpable to mankind all over this globe. For this nation has a higher mission to fulfil than the exercise of its power and beneficence on this continent. It has a mission to fulfil for humanity. I am, therefore, in favor of immediate action being taken on this question of national strength, and if need be I am for ingrafting on the fundamental law the political principles of Alexander Hamilton ; for with due regard for all other statesmen, the world affords no type, no example of a nation-builder equal to him. Talleyrand was right when he said that Hamilton was the great man of America. Marshal all the great statesmen of the world together, and let the gifted of every land speak the praise of each one according to his merit, and then call Washington and Lincoln down from heaven and ask who was the greatest statesman that ever went up from earth, and the answer from that higher life will be that Alexander Hamilton was the greatest nation-builder that ever lived among men. Then speak his praise and breathe anew his principles into our national life, and the Republic will be as enduring as the continent itself. Hamilton grasped all the nations of the earth with one sweep of the mind and erected out of feebly-connected federal association one people—an American nation. No man has enunciated such simple and yet such sublime principles of self-government as he, and no man has even approached the correctness of his principles since the Greek Solon. His was an imperial mind, not autocratic nor despotic, but all administrative and executive in its expression of political power. "He spake as never man spake." He embodied in his own organization principles of government inflexible in their application to political society, yet all-sufficient for the liberty of man. He was a child of the sea, born to rule the land.

To ingraft this Hamiltonian spirit of power into the Constitution is one of the fundamental means of national salvation which is now demanded of those charged with making and administering the laws, and no time must be lost in the execution of this great duty. The recent so-called labor strikes, sweeping over the land, made good and conservative men forget party prejudices and think anew and ask, what shall we do to be saved? That sirocco of organized violence that moved over the country was not justified in a land where the people are so young and so strong in recuperative energies, and where abound opportunities for all. But the lesson it taught must not be ignored. It must be thoughtfully considered and wisely confronted. The people must be taught that with rights and opportunities given to all, according to the measure and the capabilities of each, that whosoever falls upon this nation shall be bruised, and on whomsoever this nation falls he will be ground to atoms. Possessed as we are of all the achievements of a century, and in the face of the bright promises of the future, let no man look with indifference upon the duty of the hour; let no man say that danger is not in the brief distance. We are yet young as a nation. The violent have imperilled the rights of citizens, and "if they do these things in a green tree, what shall they do in the dry?"

Population and the complex relations of society and civilization are constantly on the increase, and any delay in making the ship of state sufficiently strong to ride triumphantly through every storm of violence hazards the perpetuity of our institutions. To save this nation is a higher duty than to serve the purposes of party. It is a duty this generation owes to the generations yet to be, far up the ascending pathway along which will

Nations step into rank,
At time's loud bugle-sound.

To accomplish these salutary ends, the following provisions of government must be established and maintained:

1. A provision for the restraint of evil-disposed persons, whether many or few;

2. A provision for the restraint of the law-makers under the Constitution; and,

3. A provision for the restraint of the officers of the law in whose charge the administration of the government is committed.

These three provisions properly observed, no difficulty lies in the way of administering self-government for the good of all the people.

With these remarks on our system of self-government as an abstract political fabric, let us pass to the co-operative relations of government and civilization.

Modern civilization has brought into the account of self-government new agencies that demand new laws for their regulation. The growth of the arts, of wealth and of population demand, under a representative form of government, regulations unknown to older forms of government. They create co-operative relations between government and civilization, and the prosperity and harmonious relations of each to the other, depending on the confidence, support and fidelity of the people, for the purposes of common good to all, beget new relations between the people and the general government, which require a wise adjustment of each interest produced by art and wealth, as well as legal relations with the government itself.

We need not go back to the origin of printing, to the birth of the telescope and the mariner's compass—inventions that opened the way for a broader and more intelligent conception of man's destiny upon the globe, and his relation to civil government. We need only begin with the steam engine—that invention that exerts all the will-power of mechanical ingenuity—that invention that has done for mechanics what the telegraph has done for human thought. Said the learned Dr. Lardner, in a lecture in Liverpool, on the power and usefulness of the steam engine : "I will eat the first steam engine that propels a vessel across the Atlantic ocean." Not more than six months passed away before an engine propelled a vessel across the Atlantic, and a new power was given to the world—a power tireless and almost omnipotent, a power that has abridged time and called men and women into new fields of activity. The steam engine is the engine of civilization. It is not limited in its power and its duties to circumstances and conditions. It labors alike for men, states and nations. It is the servant of mind and does the work of intelligence and progress. Such is the wonderful power of the steam engine. The spinning jenny comes next as an agent of civilized men. By this invention mankind was lifted from barbarism and from antique forms of traditionary customs to the condition of a new life on the Western Hemisphere. The spinning jenny gave to the world profit without labor ; it clothed the people with new garments, and necessitated new principles of government. The steam engine and the spinning jenny linked human progress with mechanical invention and opened to mankind a new field of usefulness.

It is said that the invention of the sewing machine, and its introduction in the city of New York, turned 30,000 women out of employment in that city. The sewing machine is a new agent which art has brought into use, and though small in its way, its use affected both the government and the civilization of the country. It sent poverty to the government to ask for labor, and it sent hunger to the rich man to ask for bread. But neither heeded the clamor. Both the government and the rich man left open the gates of crime, and humanity walked down to infamy, and the government and civilization moved on hand in hand, passing by on the other side, unmindful of the higher responsibility of each to the starving multitude. With the growth of invention began the growth of wealth and the growth of corporations, and these two strong, agents of wealth joined hands and grew side by side until they have become a vast power all over the land. They have widened the field of useful toil and given labor to thousands of people, yes, millions of men and women, and yet by their growth they have imposed new functions of government, the exercise of which requires new laws.

Chief among modern inventions, and the greatest one the arts have given to the world, is the railway. This new facility of commerce and travel not only transcends the ox, the mule, the horse and the steamboat in speed and usefulness, but it has also produced untold wealth in every field of its activity. As an agent of civilization there is nothing that exerts a power so demonstrative. The iron road is the road of progress, and the locomotive everywhere heralds a civilization mightier than of yore.

But a few years ago the locomotive started on the iron road to the Orient. As it entered lands where for century on century pagan superstitions had ruled mankind, it heralded a new civilization, and the world saw a new light shining from the eye of science.

The railway has grown to be a potential element in our civilization, a mighty power throughout the country, and its value is incalculable to the commerce and civilization of the people. And yet in the very hour when it is executing the labor of the people, many of those whose interests depend most upon its use, look upon the railway as an innovator, a usurper of individual rights, and the robber of the wages of honest toil. Wide-spread as this conviction may be, I hold that it is founded upon ignorance and is proclaimed by demagogues, I care not what may be their rank or what station they fill.

The telegraph may also be mentioned as an invention that exercises a great influence, both upon civilization and government. On the morning the news reached Washington City of the discovery and invention of the telegraph, a gentleman asked John C. Calhoun what he thought of it. Mr. Calhoun answered that some day it will become one of the greatest agencies of despotism in this country. I shall not undertake to say how far Mr. Calhoun was right, but the telegraph is certainly a great power, and one that has gathered to itself great wealth, and its influence and use have provoked much discussion. Viewed in any light, the telegraph exerts a great influence all over the land—an influence that reaches the government itself.

It is true that inventions and industries so wide-spread over the country, and bringing into recognition so much capital and labor as the railways and telegraphs have, do, in the very nature of things, create and will create new relations between the general government and the civilization of the people—relations more vital in their character under our form of self-government. Personal and public interests of unusual magnitude are centered in the great railways of the country, and they have become vital centres of wealth and agents of unusual power. And so rapid has been the growth of the railway system of the country that the nation now has an unconscious giant of commerce and industry to confront. And how to meet this giant of Briarean arms is a question of momentous concern to the people of this country. Not that this question is difficult to meet and solve, but that it must be met right. As an invention the railway is a promoter of civilization. No man can measure its value and usefulness, and on account of the magnitude of the railway system of the country it possesses a power which, if not rightly controlled, cannot fail to be a source of great injury to the people and the government. Power everywhere, whether in the atom or the planet, must be exerted for the right use of the thing possessing it. The railway, abstractly considered, has no power in itself, but when wielded by the agency of mind, becomes a new element in the fabric of society and government—an element so important in its use and relations as to command recognition by the government, both defensive and offensive. In other words, so great an interest and so great a power as the railway brings to our civilization must, of necessity, become a matter of national concern. The extended lines of railway, constructed and operated beyond State lines, gives them a national character, and places the power to restrain their undue use, or to defend their rights, beyond the jurisdiction of State governments. As a highway for travel and traffic, and for the transportation of soldiers and mails, the railway possesses the same inter-state character that belongs to rivers, and therefore the nation has the same jurisdiction to restrain and control the use of the railway, within such limits as may seem best for the public good. On the other hand, the railway, with all the wealth and improvements belonging to it, and the exercise of its legitimate and lawful functions, must be protected by the general government from all assaults of whatever character, or from whatever sources.

The government must, in defence of its own existence, restrain every attempt by one or more persons to interfere with the rights or interests of any part of the community. Individuals, nations and the affairs of nations must be governed by law, and the very moment disobedience is permitted to invade the rights of the people in any locality, under the constitution, the evil resulting therefrom is shared by the whole people. The body politic is analogous to the human body, and the disease or the injury that invades any part of the system or extremity of the man can not be ignored by the healthy parts.

The laws which govern and control the human being are inflexible in their operation, yet simple and all-sustaining; so, too, must be the laws that govern and control nations if those charged with making and administering the laws, desire a free and prosperous people. No matter how inflexible the national laws are that govern and control the human being, where they are rightly obeyed, men and women have more freedom in the activities of life and more mental enjoyment than when a single law is disobeyed. In fact, the disobedience of organic laws brings slavery, disease and decrepitude, and a warring of the members of the individual. If this be true, it brings us again to re-affirm our axiomatic propositions that there is no liberty but the liberty of law, and that license without the authority of law leads to anarchy. Then in vain do men talk of oppressive laws under a strong and self-adjusting constitution. A self-government is the strongest form of government in the world. When rightly adjusted to the wants and necessities of the people, each citizen becomes an integral part of the national life, a function of mental and moral power. Not so in those nations where but few persons govern. With them the people are held together by ties of blood, language, and a conviction of nationality.

NATIONAL CHARACTER IS THE OUTGROWTH OF INDIVIDUAL CHARACTER.

Again, a self-government derives much of its strength from the obedience of the people to the law, for obedience founded on a conviction of sovereignty in the individual gives strength. On the other hand, the weakness of a nation is attributable, in the main, to a failure of the people to obey the laws; or in other words, nations are enfeebled by disobedience to law. An obedient people are always a united people; a disobedient people are a disunited people. A united people are a strong people, made so by discipline and a profound conviction in favor of the government under which they live.

But we have more to consider than the simple question of a correctly organized government and an obedient and a united people. Governments, like individuals, are prone to err. They are subject to the same tendencies of good and evil that men are : and the great nation and the good nation is always born of the great and good people. As the people are, so is the nation ; and if we go back in the discussion to ask what shall we do to save the nation, the answer will be found in the answer to the question, what shall the people do to be saved? for as the people are, so is the nation. Therefore, the individual is not only a political factor in the national life, but also a moral and intellectual power. And if the people want an honest administration of government, if they want wise legislators, they must themselves be honest and wise. If we desire the nation to be founded on virtue and high purposes, the people must be virtuous and high in their bearing. This doctrine was declared by the Apostle to be ordained of Heaven. He told the Corinthians to "be not deceived; God is not mocked ; whatsoever a man soweth that shall he also reap." The same doctrine was advocated by Æschines in his speech in opposition to Athens granting Demosthenes a crown. Æschines told the Athenians that in granting crowns they judged themselves, and were forming the character of their children. Said he : "Most of all, fellow-citizens, if your sons ask whose example they shall imitate, what will you say? For you know well it is not music, nor the gymnasium, nor the schools, that mould young men ; it is much more the proclamations, the public example. If you take one whose life has no high purpose, everybody who sees it is corrupted. Beware, therefore, Athenians, remembering posterity will rejudge your judgment, and that the character of a city is determined by the character of the men it crowns." Shall we not heed the teachings of this Athenian orator and the Apostle? If we wish to have a true nation we must have a true people, actuated by a deep-rooted conviction that "righteousness exalteth a nation, but sin is a reproach to any people."

Every man and woman owes it to the nation to live a true and upright life, a life that will contribute strength and character in private and public places. This I hold to be the most important means of national salvation.

As the sea-bird seeks the rock as a refuge from the tempest and the storm, as the Christian seeks Jesus as a refuge from heaven-offending sins, so should the true man and woman, inspired with patriotism, cling to the nation for hope and happiness, giving even as they desire to receive.

CIVIL SERVICE REFORM.

But I leave this semi-social thought, and pass on to consider other means of national salvation. The present state of public affairs demands serious consideration. While it is true the nation is only in its infancy, and rapidly growing up to mature life, it is the duty of those charged with making and administering the laws to discharge their duties for the best interests of the people, and in such a manner as will give character and greatness to the nation.

The late civil conflict to eliminate slavery from our country was succeeded by the usual social and political evils, excesses and vices, that result from all wars, internecine and foreign. Corruption in office, incompetency in place has been one of the consequences, and profligacy and extravagance in every occupation of life and public duty have succeeded the late struggle to destroy slavery. The first effort of politicians and statesmen was to restore national unity and national integrity and spread over the land prosperity in every field of honest toil. How far success has been achieved in the accomplishment of these things is still undetermined. Twelve years have passed away since Lee surrendered at Appomattox Court House, and yet we hear of a "solid South" and a "solid North." There has been a constant contest for party principle, based on bitter and unnatural antagonisms—a spirit of hatred and revenge. Is it not time that the people were made prosperous by the inspiration of a new liberty, and reinvigorated by the spirit of an all-embracing national unity? But instead of such a consummation we still hear the babbling of politicians and the bitter words of partisans. Intrigue pervades every condition of official life, regardless of party principles or party power. The people have grown sick over the politicians' clamor about civil service reform. For almost a decade this pretense of reform has been heralded over the country as a panacea for theft and incompetency in official life. The pretence for such a reform had its origin in a few men who sought to establish a kind of American kid-glove aristocracy, and at best it was intended for clerks below the age of twenty years, and not for party slaves who have grown corrupt in their service. There never was anything in civil service reform, and there never can be anything in it as presented by its advocates. The American people are a democratic people : in official life they can only recognize distinctions made by competency and fidelity. The capable and qualified man is the true official reformer. He is the man for the place, and if party usages demand official changes, those in office have only to substitute men of equal qualifications. This is the only reform the American people demand for official life.

THE FINANCIAL QUESTION ; AN AMERICAN SYSTEM OF COMMERCE.

Let us now pass to financial reform. To meet the financial exigencies precipitated by the rebellion, the government was compelled to use its credit to the utmost extent. It issued currency for the people, and bonds for home and foreign markets. It created a cancer of an incurable debt, if perpetuated under the law upon which it is founded.

Let us confront the financial problem of the country, for this is the great problem that affects the interests and prosperity of the people. To consider this question properly I desire to state : First, that the financial affairs of every nation are founded upon principles of a local and distinctive national character and necessity. Second, that every nation has the same right to organize its own system of finance without reference to other nations, as it has to enact laws and to fix the qualification of citizenship. I further hold that it is a fundamental principle upon which the financial affairs of every nation are based, that debt and credit must be founded upon the resources, labor and skill of the people of a country— conditions peculiarly local and special. I further hold that a nation has the right to fix a standard, not of value, but of payment, and to make it out of such material as it may select itself, and that, too, without any reference to the financial affairs of any other nation. I further hold that money in essence is that which the law makes money. It is a creature of law, designed for a facility in the transaction of business. There has been as much foolish discussion about what money is as there has been about the fabled tempter of the human race. I therefore repeat again, that money is in essence that which the law makes money. Nothing else is money, and nothing else can be money. We hear men speak about money being a measure of value. I do not so understand it. Money, technically speaking, is neither a measure nor weight of value, but a denomination, a token of power and standard of payment. It is made of fractional denominations and is based upon numbers and not on weights and measures or the value of the material of which it is composed ; and when we consider the definition of money, with the fact that it only represents value by means of cents, dimes and dollars, how is it possible to clothe it with any other worth than that which the law gives it?

Then if it is a creature of law, why does not a nation have the same right to make its own money as it has to enact its own laws? Secretary Sherman said a man was a fool who said a dollar could be made of paper. This certainly is a very low expression for a man to make to more than 40,000,000 people, most of whom believe to the contrary, and whose industries are prostrated by the stupidity and anti-American policy of the Secretary of the United States Treasury. Even gold is not money unless the law makes it money. If it has an intrinsic value because of its scarcity, it can only be sold by weight, as iron and brass are sold. It has no other market value until the power of the law touches it and gives it a money value.

Now, if it be true that a nation has the right to make its own money—and I challenge human reason and the honesty of mankind to controvert it—then are not those charged with making the laws bound by every obligation that legislators can possibly be under, to the people, to organize such a system of finance and make such money as the needs of the country demand, and such as will give labor and prosperity to the people?

As to the material out of which to make money, there ought not to be a question of dispute, any more than there is about the question how to make bread. Nobody can object to the government making money out of gold or silver. But the law-makers and the administrators of the laws of this government have no more right to say that the sovereignty of the law cannot make a paper dollar represent one hundred cents as well as the gold or silver dollar, than they have to say that a yard-stick made of pine wood does not contain thirty-six inches, as well as if made of box-wood, gold or silver. The principle is precisely the same. Mathematical science and a conventionality has fixed thirty-six inches for one yard, and one hundred cents for one dollar ; but mathematical science does not say what kind of material shall represent the inches and the cents. These are matters for economy and the public interests to determine. Now as to what material our American money should be made of is purely a question of public interest and convenience.

But the gold-monger says, if you make money of paper, there is danger of getting too much of it. In answer, I would first ask if nature has been prodigate in supplying too much air and too much water for man's use, and if there is a superabundance, is anybody harmed by it? I suspect that if man had been commissioned from on high to make air and water, his selfishness would have limited the quantity and the amount, so that the rich could have an abundance and the poor scarcely enough to breathe and drink. But the good Father above spread air and water

around the earth, on hill-tops and in pastures, for the free use of all.
Who ever heard of too much food in a country injuring the interests of
the people, and how can a wise and liberal supply of money injure the
business interests of the people or the country? When there is more
food the poor people get more to eat, and when there is more money the
poor people get more of it. Plenty of money does not injure a house,
it don't harm a railway nor a printing office.

I sometimes think in moments of reflection, when I contemplate the
present and the future of America, that a God ought to come from heaven
to teach the people and administer the government. We have a precedent in Italian literature. A God abandoned heaven to live in Italy,
Apollo fled from Olympus to dwell in Aussonia. Here we have a vast
continental nation, and it does really seem that there is no public man
bold enough to rise above the demagogueism of the politician, and declare
the destiny of the nation and prescribe laws for the better government of
the people.

Planting myself upon the fundamental fact that money in essence is
that which the law makes money, I hold that it is the bounden duty of
the American nation to so legislate as to relieve the American people of
the weight of the national debt. A debt so enormous, put upon a people
so young, and held there by a government that does so little to relieve
the burdens of taxation, engenders discontent and distrust throughout the
land. A system of American finance ought to be organized for this
nation. It must be a system founded upon the necessities and interests
of the American people. It must be a system of finance that will give
to the people a real genuine American money, without any reference to
whether it is adapted to the speculative uses of any nation of Europe.

I would make American money of paper and impress upon it the
sovereign power of the nation. Metal money made of gold is a heathen
relic—a calf that was once worshipped by idolaters. Upon the white wings
of paper the thoughts of the human race, of the greatest and best of
mankind, are carried and heralded to every land. The world can live
without gold, but blot paper from the earth and you can only do one
thing worse, and that is to blow out the light of the sun. Think for one
moment what a calamity it would be to blot paper from the earth. Consider such an event for one moment, and I challenge the world to prove
that there is more intrinsic value in gold than in paper. Think what a
meaning there is in the fact that the world can do without gold, but it
cannot do without paper. Think of it, you heathen devotees, as you stand
with your thoughts and convictions away back of the thirteenth century,

at the opening of which a new light began to dawn from the West upon the world. Think of it, and then say shall America's progress be clogged by your devotion to gold, when paper is the white-winged evangel of the nineteenth century?

We want a money that will turn the wheels of toil, that will give life to industry and activity to commerce—a money that will inspire confidence and devotion in the people for the government under which they live.

By one of the terms of this American system, let it be provided that at least $100,000,000 worth of the bonds be called in annually and paid off with our American money. Give Europe our money and her people will invest in this country in building railways and in developing mines, and other needed improvements. Let this money be the money of the nation, and, backed by the will and demands of the people, the people will vote for such a money ; it will buy their bread and meat, their clothing, and pay taxes, and in defence of such a money will the people fight.

How simple, and yet how great, would such a financial system be ! Give to the country an American system of finance, and you at once give the nation a new standing among the governments of the world. O how disgraceful is the sad spectacle to-day ! Here we have a continental nation, larger in its available territorial domain than any nation on the earth. It has more natural resources, more navigable advantages, and more intelligence among its people than can be found elsewhere on the globe. It is the land of Washington, Franklin, Webster, Calhoun, Clay, Benton and Lincoln, and yet through misjudged legislation, it stands before the courts of the world as a third-rate power. Its diplomatic officials are disgraced in every land, by the poverty-stricken compensation paid for their services. Its financial policy has chained it to Europe. Metal money means Europe, the money power of the world, and America on her knees to Europe. Europe owns and directs Wall street, and Wall street controls the Washington government, and the Washington government has the Valley of the Mississippi bound hand and foot. And yet in the very face of these things, when the land is full of bread, thousands go hungry, because there is no labor whereby to earn bread. The Secretary of the Treasury tells the people that the government has nothing to do with the hard times. What think ye of such a declaration? He further adds, that the government is not responsible for good or bad crops. In answer, I have to say that hard or prosperous times are not always incident to good or bad crops.

Alexander Hamilton, whom Secretary Sherman has succeeded

— 29 —

in office, held quite a different opinion on the subject of the government diffusing prosperity among the people. He entered the Treasury office when the new States were prostrated in poverty and weakness, without skill and without inventions. By the aid of the government he soon lifted the people of the new States to prosperity and power; so, too, can this administration do if it had a man equal to Alexander Hamilton for Secretary of the Treasury. One of the great needs of the nation is a governmental policy adapted to the wants of America and her theory of government, and not for the interest of Europe. All our legislation should be so shaped, to make this nation great, and build it up as the American nation. But sad enough, the whole financial policy of the Washington government has been for ten years in favor of Europe. The hope of the world is in America, and it is for American statesmen to legislate for America and not for Europe. An examination of the map of the world demonstrates that there are but two nations on the globe, north of the equator, which, if compelled to live and confine their commerce to their own territory, could exist one year without being reduced to anarchy; these two nations are America and China. There is not a nation on the continent of Europe that possesses within itself the resources and recuperative energies to live alone. Hence the nations of Europe must of necessity draw their life-blood from other people in other lands, and the efforts of American statesmen are to contribute to Europe instead of building up America.

THE REMOVAL OF THE NATIONAL CAPITAL, AND WHERE TO LOCATE IT.

The next step in the discussion in favor of national salvation is the adjustment of the government to the topographical conditions of the continent of North America. As there is a law governing the right adjustment of the paternal home, and the public improvements to the domestic habitation, so too is there a law governing the right adjustment of the home of the government, from which will emanate the laws of the country, according to the topographical character of the continent.

He who builds a palace or a cottage must lay the foundation according to the ground on which he decides to build. He adjusts all the structure according to the surroundings and according to the necessities of the improvement; so, too, must be the rules observed in establishing the fabric of government on the territory where it is designed to exist. When civilization clothes the country with population and wealth, the log cabin erected in the wilderness must give place to the palace designed for the permanent abode of the domestic household.

If we desire the perpetuity of this nation we must consider the topographical character of the country over which the Constitution now and henceforth is designed to extend, and re-locate the capital of the nation—the home of the government—in accordance with the topographical character of the whole country and in respect to the future growth of population and power. When the government consisted of the thirteen original States, and six of them not as large as the State of Missouri, the present seat of government was selected in accordance with the dictates of wisdom. Our fathers legislated for themselves according to their best judgment, and in harmony with the topographical character of the thirteen States of the then Federal Government. Near one century has passed away since the capital was located at its present place, and the nation now extends almost over a vast, wide continent. It has almost trebled in the number of its States, and has almost twelve times the population. But more than all those, the topographical character of the country, over which the Constitution now extends, demands a re-location of the national capital, a re-adjustment of the government to the continent over which the national fabric extends. Politicians, demagogues and fools may laugh at the thought of removing the capital to the Valley of the Mississippi, where it will be safe against both foreign and domestic foes, and from whence the laws will reach with equal vigor to every extremity of the country. He who ignores the idea that there is nothing in the adjustment of a self-government to the topographical character of the country over which it extends, denies the existence of constitutional conditions that regulate things with each other ; and he who denies that the re-location of the national capital at some central and appropriate place in the Valley of the Mississippi is not of vital concern to the perpetuity of this nation, has given but little thought to the under-life principles upon which this nation is to stand and endure.

Said Mr. Madison : "An equal attention to the rights of the community is the basis of republics. If we consider, sir, the effects of legislative power on the aggregate community, we must feel equal inducements to look for the centre in order to find the present seat of government. Those who are most adjacent to the seat of legislation will always possess advantages over others. An earlier knowledge of the laws, a greater influence in enacting them, and a thousand other circumstances, will give a superiority to those who are thus situated. If we consider the influence of the government in its executive department, there is no less reason to conclude that it ought to be placed in the centre of the Union. It ought to be in a situation to command information from every part of the Union, to watch every conjecture, to seize every circumstance that can be improved. The executive eye ought to be placed where it can best see the dangers which threaten, and the executive arm whence it may be extended most effectually to the protection of every part. In the judiciary department, if it is not equally necessary, it is highly important that the government should be equally accessible to all.''

The friends of capital removal want no better argument than was made by Mr. Madison. But of course there is a class of men who are very deep in shallow matters and very shallow in deep matters, who say that telegraphs and railways render communication so easy and universal that it does not matter where the capital is located. Now I admit the usefulness of both these agencies, but whatever argument there is in them applies much better to almost any city of any considerable size in the Valley of the Mississippi than it does to Washington City. I undertake to say that there is not a sane man beneath the shining sun that can make a sensible argument in favor of the capital of this nation remaining at Washington. In reference to where the capital ought to be re-located, it was agreed among the friends of capital removal, eight years ago, that no locality should be presented until official steps were taken for removal. I have until the present adhered to that agreement, but now and henceforth I propose to advocate a locality for the future capital of the United States, and that locality comprises a district ten or twenty miles square, covering the region of country where the great rivers of this continent unite and blend their waters together; where the Illinois, the Mississippi and Missouri rivers join together to send their united waters to the sea. At that place centres more than 20,000 miles of available navigable waters, and near by centres the largest railway system on the continent. That locality is the pelvic region in the physical organization of this continent : it is the golden mean .where the zones of the North and the South meet. It combines the greatest physical power on the globe, and the navigable rivers that meet there form a stronger bond of national unity than the Constitution itself. The best water in the world flows from the Rocky Mountains through the Missouri. Material for food, clothing and building purposes can there be gathered in greater abundance and cheaper than at any other point on the continent. And there Missouri and Illinois can unite and give a home to the government of this imperial Republic of States— a capital worthy the nation, the symbol of whose power it is.

"The Valley of the Mississippi is the chosen seat of population and power on this continent.'' It is the only section of the country that can stand alone. The Atlantic States can never secede for want of food, nor the Pacific States for want of the metals. Powerful enough in numbers to make the laws of the Republic, the people of the Valley will also be powerful enough to enforce them.

This valley has already demonstrated its power in the late rebellion. When the struggle opened, Gen. Scott commanded the army; Gen. Dix, of New York, commanded that department: Gen. Butler, of Massachusetts, commanded in Baltimore; Gen. McClellan, of New York, commanded the department of Ohio, and Gen. Lyon, of Connecticut, the department of Missouri—all Eastern men. When the war closed, Gen. Grant, of Illinois, was at the head of the army; Gen. Sherman, of Missouri, had brought his Western army into North Carolina; Gen. Thomas, of Ohio, had command in Tennessee, and Gen. Sheridan, of Ohio, was Grant's favorite subordinate in the army before Richmond—all Western men.

No foreign invader can ever penetrate the Valley of the Mississippi. On the eastward the Atlantic States form an impregnable fortification to resist any invader, while the Alleghany mountains shut in the valley from attack. On the westward the Pacific States would resist an invader, and the Sierras and plains arrest his march. On the north, regions impassable in summer by reason of water, and in winter by reason of snows, shut in the valley from approach; while from the Gulf coast, as experience in the war of 1812 and in the recent civil war abundantly proved, there is no pathway northward which could not easily be held against any invading force. Then defended on all sides with ample water facilities, reaching throughout the whole interior, for the transportation of forces toward any threatened point, the people of the valley are more secure from an invasion than those of any nation on earth.

These things being true, I now affirm that it is the bounden duty of those charged with making and administering the laws to re-locate the home of the government, the capital of the nation, in the Valley of the Mississippi, without delay. Until this is done, unnatural national troubles will continue to disturb the body politic, and men will continue to talk of a solid North and a solid South, and elements of discord will pervade the people of the nation because of the unnatural adjustment of the government to the topographical character of the country.

But the capital removed to the Valley States, they will cement around it, and the nation will throb with a new life, and perfect peace and perfect union will henceforth be constant and enduring.

If the American people hesitate to take this step, they will do so with peril to the general government, for no power in the world can prevent the capital from being removed west. This is a government of majorities, and the majority will not go forever over the Alleghanies to make laws to govern themselves, nor will the people of the Valley of the Mississippi submit to a government that strives to promote the interests of the European capitalists to the detriment of their own honor, their industry, and the humiliation of their government.

UNJUST DISCRIMINATIONS BY THE NATIONAL BUREAU OF STATISTICS AGAINST ST. LOUIS AND THE SOUTH-WEST.

But recently the Washington Bureau of Statistics issued a volume on the internal commerce of the country, and one would suppose that the government of the United States would not issue a partial work in reference to the affairs of its own people. But the compiler of that volume, although compelled to present the great preponderance of internal over external commerce, so arranged the whole drift of the book as to show the currents of trade running to the Atlantic seaboard, and nearly every map in it discriminates against St. Louis and the South-west. In mapping the trunk railways belonging to the St. Louis system, several lines are left off of the map entirely. The commercial channels of the cities of the West whose interests are regarded as being more allied to the Atlantic seaboard are fully presented. But this is not all. Secretary Sherman, in his speech in Ohio, also took an opportunity to make a thrust at Western commerce. I undertake to say that the manner in which he presented the tonnage of the three great trunk railways leading to the Atlantic seaboard is false. In estimating the tonnage on either of those three great lines of road, he forgets that he is estimating freight all the way from San Francisco, Galveston, New Orleans, the Yellowstone and every part of the West, the tonnage of which freight has already been counted several times on connecting lines of road. On the other hand, the Mississippi and its tributaries float annually a commerce valued at $200,000,000, and they are more valuable as commercial thoroughfares than all the railroads in the country; and say what men will, the people of the Mississippi Valley will henceforth go out at the Gulf of Mexico with their surplus commerce designed for the markets of the world.

The genius of Capt. Eads, our own citizen of the valley, has contrived one of the important means to achieve this destiny in harmony with nature herself, and do what the world may, or what nations will, there is but one destiny for the people of this grand valley.

THE STRIKES.

I now pass to consider some of the questions of the future as they relate to what has gone before, as means of national salvation.

America is the land of the future. Here are to be solved all the great questions of government and civilization. It therefore becomes the American statesmen to go beyond the lessons of to-day, and think wisely on the questions of the future. The one great thought of the American citizen should be how to build upon this continent an imperial Republic of States, over-arched by a constitution that rules from ocean to ocean ·and from zone to zone—a constitution that derives its efficacy and its power from "we, the people of the United States."

The first lesson that presents itself for consideration is derived from the late so-called "labor strikes." Last July a civilized sirocco swept over the land from the Atlantic ocean to the Mississippi river. The American people were confronted, in almost a day, with a sweeping social tornado that seemed to threaten ruin both to civilization and government, and men everywhere were asking, "what shall we do to be saved?" Bitter partisans forgot their political creed, and men met each other face to face and inquired if there was not something in the teachings of the founders of the nation, irrespective of party, still wanting to make our government strong and enduring. The authority of the law was defied, human life was imperiled, and the wealth of generations threatened by a lawless and misguided people. It was called a labor strike, and many men who ought to have been wiser shared in the insanity of the hour.

Since the smoke of the battle has cleared away and reason has a hearing, I undertake to say that the late strikes did not have their origin in a want of bread, nor in a want of higher wages. These assumptions were only pretexts for a rupture. If we go deep in the condition of things we find that in the physical world earthquakes and storms are constantly taking place, the causes of which do not have their origin in the earth where the concussion is, nor in the wind out of which the storm is made. The earth and the wind are the means, but not the cause, of the shock and the storm. The cause lies back of both; so, too, in the social world, where mind operates upon physical conditions. Such is the nature of man, that most of the social disorders have their origin in a pretext. Those founded on a principle, or having their origin in a principle, never accomplish that for which it is claimed they are designed. A few years ago a wide-spread agitation swept over the country in the name, and ostensibly in favor of, woman suffrage. I undertake to say the cause that produced that agitation did not have its origin in the constitution of human nature, for the purpose of establishing woman suffrage. It grew out of an under-life social principle, designed to accomplish a great social change in the organic condition of human society, far different from woman suffrage.

But rising nearer to the surface of human action, it is not unusual for one man, or many men, to take advantage of a pretext to precipitate an attack upon some persons or corporations, with the pretence of redressing some imaginary wrong. The cause of the late strikes had its origin far back, and is the result of a growing falsehood. It is a well ascertained fact that the wages of railway engineers and other railway employees are at least 30 to 40 per cent. higher since the war than before it, and that the cost of living is only six to eight per cent. higher than before the war. Railway engineers were paid on the Illinois Central Railway $2.70 per day up to January 1st, 1862. Wages were then raised to $3.30, and continued at that rate through the war. They now run from $3.75 to $4 per day.

In the face of such facts, what earthly reason was there for a strike? There was none. The war brought upon the country extravagance and vice, and with the spread of vice, labor in many fields of toil contracted, while all men's wants increased; unbalanced relations grew up between capital and labor, and vice and extravagance demanded more money to satisfy their wants. There is scarcely a man in the land who does not spend more in extravagance than he did before the war, and the want of money to meet this extravagance creates a pretext for those who are banded together, and a strike is precipitated in the name of the want for bread.

No want for bread has yet occurred in this land of America. The world has no evidence that the American people have ever wanted for bread, and it is a slander on America for any man to say that her people have wanted for bread since Columbus came to her shores. In this discussion I desire to bring to my aid the support of the Rev. Richard Coldley, of Flint, Michigan, whose words are as true as steel and as bright as gold. "We have been counting it as one of the achievements of our civilization, that every man may absolutely control his own. No man shall be forced to sell, and no man shall be forced to buy ; no man shall be forced to work against his will, or for a person he does not like, or for a price that does not suit him. If a man has a bushel of wheat, he may set his price on it, and keep it until he can get his price. But he may not compel another man to buy it, nor prevent his neighbor from selling for less. If a man has a day's labor, he may set his own price on it and refuse to work till he can get his price, but may not compel another to employ him, nor prevent his neighbor from working for less. If these principles are wrong, then our whole social system is wrong, and the entire process of thought for the last five hundred years has been drifting the wrong way, and must be reversed. That process of thought and experience has been steadily toward entire individual freedom.

" The judgment of the civilized world—a judgment growing more clear and consistent and decided as experience has justified its soundness—that judgment is, that in the long run, and in the broadest scope, it is wisest and best that every man should dispose of his own as best he may. That judgment, growing up in the progress of history, is going to stand, and will be applied more and more thoroughly and consistently as it is understood.

"The outcome of the late strike illustrates the power of truth. Had these men been right, they would have been resistless. They would have created a revolution if they could have appealed to the moral sense of men, or even their own moral sense. But their attitude was plainly wrong, and the good sense of the great country soon crystallized about the truth, and took form against them. Their own better judgment recoiled, and their front was broken by concussion with the truth."

I have stated this whole matter just as the facts demonstrate, but in so doing I do not say that the laboring men are all wrong, and those who own and operate railways are right; I do not say this. for it is impossible for power and wealth, uncontrolled by well tested experience and just laws, to not err; men who own and operate railways have the same passions, appetites and propensities as men who labor, and are liable to err, and to even do injustice. But the laboring man's remedy is not in striking, his crime is striking ; there is no law civil or divine that will justify any one or more men in attacking in an unlawful manner any principle of human society which applies alike to all. Let me illustrate. There is no branch of human toil under our form of government, and no official position, that is not open to every citizen of the government ; therefore where it is possible for a railway engineer to inherit $200,000 or $300,000, thus enabling him to buy railway stock, or build a railway, and thereby secure the presidency of the company, such engineer has no moral or legal right to make war upon any man because he holds a position above him.

I am confident there is a spirit of justice pervading our entire social and political fabric that will not long delay in correcting any injustice that may be done to any class of our people, and in any field of toil. Time is the evil genius that stands between capital and labor; capital can wait, labor cannot, and herein lies the secret of the contest. But labor will regulate its own wages, just as the ebb and flow of prosperity regulates the rents of the rich man. To fix a standard of wages all over this country in any field of toil is as impossible as to fix a standard of height for all men. Labor must be regulated as all other questions are, by some fundamental principles. It has never been a question among men how to prevent too much work, hence the principle upon which to found labor must be full work and full pay. The laborer must own himself and work according to his own wants and inclination; I therefore pronounce the eight-hour law both unwise and a source of vast evil to the country. I so told Charles Sumner when the Senate was taking the vote. He voted against it. Now the clamor of the so-called laboring men is for full wages for eight hours' labor. The government ought to repeal the law and re-enact a higher law, making full work and full pay the law for him who owns and him who earns.

One of the great difficulties now before the country is the opportunity for fools and demagogues. The clamor of the mob inspires their patriotism and humanity, and they at once become statesmen of uncommon wisdom and ability. They talk of laboring men as if they were an especial class of men from whom God Almighty withheld his decree, that "by the sweat of the brow shalt thou eat bread all the days of thy life." The laboring man is he who works in any field of honest toil, no matter whether he carries a hod or runs a ship across the sea, no matter whether he plows the sod or executes the law, no matter whether he watches a herd on the plains of Chaldea or helps to build a tower of Babel.

I would like to tell the demagogue who is so willing to espouse a cause about which he knows nothing, that there is no labor question that is not also a question of government, of commerce and civilization, and that when he consents to be a patriot for the purpose of getting an office he ought to remember that all our labor and commercial interests are so blended with our civilization that " one touch of nature makes all akin."

The men that build the locomotives are not the men that strike. The men who strike are the men who band themselves together for that purpose. The one fundamental purpose of the Brotherhood of Engineers is to take law and the rights of others in their own hands when any pretext arises to give them an opportunity.

When English cabs were first put on the locomotives on the Baltimore and Ohio Railway the engineers struck; they refused to work until the cabs were taken off. They said if the locomotive should run off of the track they could not escape from danger. They would now strike again if the cabs were taken off. The same law governs all people who band themselves in any form of human organization. Such become clannish, tyrannical, dictatorial and jealous of others. I care not what the organization may be, whether in the name of labor or religion, or secret societies, or anything else. Give me the man that has sufficient manhood to trust all his rights and interests and the rights and interests of his family to citizenship, and to the laws of his country, then give me the nation that is made of such men, and hate and hypocrisy will leave the earth.

THE GROWTH OF POPULATION.

I now pass to consider the growth of population under our Constitution. According to Malthus, any people well fed and well clad and clothed will double their numbers every thirty-three and a third years; according to George Combe, we double every twenty-five years, and according to Dr. Elder, we double every twenty-three and a half years. Taking either estimate for a standard of authority, we shall have near one hundred million of population at the close of this century, and the child is now born who will see over four hundred million of population subsisting in plenty and comfort under our Constitution. The predominant blood of our population is that masterful Anglo-Saxon, which has made Germany the most powerful of European nations, and England the queen of commerce and the mistress of the seas. In the language of another: "It is a remarkable fact that the several successive streams of westward migration of the white Aryan race, from the primitive Paradise, in the neighborhood of the primeval cities of Sogd and Balkh, in High Asia, long separated in times of migration, and for the most part distinct in the European areas finally occupied by them, and which, in the course of its grand march of twenty thousand years or more, has created nearly the whole of the civilization, arts, sciences and literature of this globe, building seats of fixed habitation and great cities, successively, in the rich valleys of the Ganges, the Euphrates, the Nile, the rivers and isles of Greece, the Tiber and the Po, the Danube, the Rhine, the Elbe, the Seine and Thames, wandering children of the same great family, are now, in these latter times, brought together again in their descendants and representatives, Semitic, Pelasgic, Celtic, Teutonic, and Sclavonic, here in the newly discovered common land of promise, and are commingled (especially in this great Valley of the Mississippi) into one common brotherhood of race, language, law and liberty."

The native races found on this continent afford ample evidence of the adaptation of the physical condition of the country to produce a united and homogeneous people. In its population many races are represented, but all are fusing and blending into one compact nation, and soon the world will behold on this continent a new and superior type of man, an American type wrought out of the best blood of all other races. Then, contemplating the future growth of population under our supreme law, are we not admonished to look deeper into the constitution of our national life, and meet face to face the new and confronting problems? Must we not look wisely and timely to the means of national salvation essential to the perpetuity of the Republic and the maintenance of our civilization? We must not be blind to the fact that with succeeding years we shall be compelled to pass through most of the experience incident to other and former nations.

As there is no ship that does not meet a stormy sea, so there is no nation that does not have its difficulties to encounter. But I believe if we choose wisdom, justice, intelligence, humanity and power with which to try and determine all our national questions, that no serious trouble will befall us for a thousand years to come. National strength is our greatest hope.

God forbid that any future Sesostris, another Attila, Alaric or Tamerlane will be born of the follies and failures of the American people and let loose to deluge this land with blood and plant the banner of misguided ambition on the graves of our fathers. I want no communes imported to this country by deck passage to be permitted to band together with lawless intent to destroy the wealth of generations of honest toil. We can avert such fatalities if we act wisely and timely.

THE TEXAS PACIFIC RAILWAY.

Already duties of vital concern to the nation demand execution. Our country must be built up. A nation, like a steam engine, must have safety-valves. It is not enough in the establishment of government, to alone fix restraints on the people, and on the law-makers, and those charged with the duty of administering the laws, but beyond all these, it is the duty of a nation to provide for the redundancy of its population, and such provisions may be denominated national safety-valves. Already such is the prostration of our industry, that thousands of our population are out of employment, and it is the bounden duty of the government to open avenues of labor to those able and willing to work.

The first step in this direction, and the first step to relieve the country of hard times, is for Congress to repeal the resumption act, and then pass the Texas Pacific Railway Bill. For Congress to refuse to build that road, is to do an injustice to one section of the country to favor another section. The South sent out the Alabama upon the high seas to prey upon the commerce of this country, but that vessel did more to build up the North than all the banks of England. It drove capital from the seas, it unlocked the capital of the sea-board cities, and sent it out over the Northwestern States to build bridges, foundries, factories and railroads. That vessel exerted the influence that bridged every river and connected every city in the Northwest by rail, and achieved in the building of the Pacific Railway the greatest commercial event of our generation. The building of the Texas Pacific will add to the national wealth and to the national character a thousand-fold more than it will cost. It will give labor to many thousands of unemployed men, and plant the seeds of empire on the frontier, that will soon spread our constitution over the city of Montezuma. Five thousand men at work on the Texas Pacific will soon found a colony in Mexico.

The endorsement by the general government of the bonds of the Texas Pacific, will give 5,000 men immediate employment.

The nation owes the Texas Pacific Road to the South. It owes it to that region of country to which and over which a great wave of Saxon blood will soon move in its course to the tropical lands and waters of the Western Hemisphere. Thitherward are our people looking, and thither will they go. The next great movement of our population will be southward.

THE IMPROVEMENT OF THE MISSISSIPPI RIVER AND ITS TRIBUTARIES.

There is still another work of incalculable value to our national growth and to the commerce of the country—the improvement of the Mississippi river and its tributaries. I have it from the ablest railway man in the valley of the Mississippi, that if the Mississippi river and its tributaries were rightly improved, they would be more valuable to the commerce of the Mississippi Valley than all the railways in it. If a work so great and so important presents itself to the nation, must we not insist that Congress shall rise to the dignity of the duty, and establish a vast system of river improvements? Let us have a great national highway, a great ship-river, from Chicago, St. Louis,′ Pittsburg and Omaha to the Gulf of Mexico. Let us make the rivers worthy the respect and use of the nation, and fit channels through which to transport our commerce to the sea.

These two important works, the building of the Texas Pacific Railway and the improvement of the Mississippi and its tributaries, are now demanded of the general government. Besides being great safety-valves to the nation, they will add incalculable wealth to the country. It is therefore the bounden duty of Congress to order both to be done.

A LARGE STANDING ARMY.

Beyond these present urgent demands upon the government to provide labor for the unemployed population, there are still other safety-valves which must be provided for future security. It may be found necessary to create a large standing army, which would absorb many unemployed persons every year. A nation must have a police force as well as a city. I think it is not difficult to prove that it is far cheaper for a city to have a strong police force than to not have one. If this be true, I think it can also be demonstrated that a nation ought to have a police or a standing army. Power, with the ability for decisive action, never was an element of danger in any nation, but always a guarantee of safety. In view of the great future of this country, and the necessity of maintaining the peace and the prosperity of the people, it is all-important that those charged with making the laws should provide the means for national safety in advance of danger. To create a large army will require no infringement on our republican institutions. The government must possess full power to put down all troubles of whatever character, and in whatever part of the county, and without any regard to state and municipal authorities, referring only the duty first to local authority without permitting red tape or party interference to stand in the way. It must be given the power to control telegraph lines and railways from the very moment banded organizations, with intent of violence, begin to inaugurate trouble. If the telegraphic news about the strikes last July had been withheld from the public press, the trouble would not have grown half so formidable. Another national safety-valve could be established by the inauguration by the general government of a system of public works. There are great parks over the continent that ought to be improved. Labor thus directed would call into requisition many unemployed people. Timber ought to be cultivated on the plains and artesian wells made. Such work would afford labor for many years to come.

THE LABOR QUESTION OF THE FUTURE.

I now desire to go back in the discussion and call your attention to the fact that there is a muttering in the storm, a social earthquake in the future. There is unconsciously a great and a real labor question growing up in the future, and in the language of another, " I desire to speak to you of human powers and of human sufferings ; of the powers and the sufferings, not of the selected few to whom fortune has assigned property and station, and along with these, voice and influence in the world's councils ; but of the Children of Labor, of the millions who say little and do much, by whom the world is fed and clothed, by whom cities are built and forests subdued, and deserts reclaimed. I desire to speak of those whose strong arms ceaselessly tugging at the oar, have impelled through all time the bark of life ; and briefly to ask of the Past how it has treated them ; of the Present, what is their actual condition ; of the Future, what may be their coming fate ?"

"There is no real wealth in this world but the labor of man. Were the mountains made of gold and the valleys of silver, the world would not be one grain of corn the richer; no one comfort would be added to the human race. In consequence of our consideration for the precious metals, one man is enabled to heap to himself luxuries at the expense of the necessaries of his neighbors."

In the organization of human society, and especially under a representative form of government, each man and woman still retains, as in a state of nature, his or her individuality, with the right to make the best they can of themselves under the circumstances. If one man is stronger than another, he is entitled to what his strength will bring. If one woman is more industrious than another, she is entitled to what her industry will bring her. And so each one is entitled to the best use of the gifts of nature. But often a superior gift unfits a person to use another faculty, and if human society and the distribution of labor does not afford the individual an opportunity to use his best gift, then civilization is likely to inflict a penalty upon such and compel them to want. But in every land and under all forms of government there is a limit to opportunity and to occupation. This opens a wide field for contest, and gives to one man advantages over another. It constantly widens the gulf between opportunity and occupation on one side, and effort and want on the other side. These grow into two extremes of human society and forces upon all populous countries the one great condition of mankind, which becomes the human problem of the world, viz: That as civilization advances, the masses darken and decline. How to prevent this condition of human society has been the study of the social architects of the world. And so long as human society and human governments are so organized as to limit occupation and opportunity, so long will the vast horde clamor for bread, and that, too, in a land of plenty.

I readily admit that it is utterly impossible to establish human equality among men. It cannot be done among the trees, the rivers, nor the stars. But it can be more nearly approached among the world's people, because they are endowed with reason, aspiration and a sense of justice. And while it is true that a man and woman born into the world must stand upon the individuality and capabilities of each, with but two principles of right upon which to stand— viz: mine and thine—the very moment society and government is organized, a new principle enters into the account of human relations, a third interest—our interest, or the public interest. Under a system of civilization based upon a craving, selfish and ambitious individuality, that permits the big fish to eat up the little ones, the third or public interest is based almost wholly on the rights and protection of property. Under such a system men are far more indifferent about securing and protecting the lives and happiness of each, than they are about the protection of the property of each. The palaces, ships, and commercial houses, which are the creation of labor alone, are more guarded than human lives and human happiness.

I do not object to wealth; on the contrary, I would do all in my power to promote the growth of wealth on this continent and in our great cities. But unless the human mind is ameliorated by the growth of the intellectual and moral faculties, men will grow selfish in the accumulation of property, and forget that want and misery are begging for bread and for comfort, even unto death.

I do not dream of the millenium, but I do look forward to the day when this grasping, heartless civilization under which we now live, and which is founded upon unconscious individuality, will be supplanted by a social order founded upon humanity and the public good. A civilization that plants no faith in blood. A civilization, the efforts of which will be so blended with the purposes of the government as to unfold a new manifestation of public life ; which will secure to every citizen living under the constitution happiness and comfort, and the security of life as well as the protection of property. I believe the day is not distant when wealth will be made, in a degree, responsible for poverty, and that intelligence will be made responsible for ignorance.

To-day poverty and ignorance cost more than they ought. They beget crime and fill poor-houses, jails and penitentiaries, and load society with unnecessary burdens. And yet for all these evils we fall back on the labor question and then charge the government and society for sins of omission and commission.

Now I believe that under our constitution, and on this continent, this question can be met and solved. It will cost far less to solve it than to leave it unsolved, and its solution would be a sublime achievement for humanity and for this nation. Said Carlyle : " The saddest sight under the sun is to see a man able and willing to work, thence lacking the necessaries of life because there is no work to do. Hunger begets in man a grim monster. The hungry man doubts the favor of God, and turns wickedly upon his fellows and braves all law to get bread."

THE GREAT NATION OF FUTURITY.

I now pass to the last part of the discussion—the great nation of futurity and the party of the future.

"Our national birth was the beginning of a new history, the formation and progress of an untried political system, which separates us from the past and connects us with the future only ; and so far as regards the natural rights of man, in moral, political and national life, we may confidently assume that our country is destined to be the great nation of futurity." It is so destined because the principle upon which a nation is organized fixes its destiny, and that of equality is perfect, is universal. It presides in all the operations of the physical world, and it is also the conscious law of the soul, the self-evident dictate of morality, which accurately defines the duty of man to man, and consequently of man's rights as man. I confidently believe that on this continent is growing up the great nation and the great people of the world. The expansive future is our arena and for our history. We are entering on its untrodden space; we are the nation of human progress, and who will, what can set limits to our onward march? The far-reaching, the boundless future will be the era of American greatness. In our future growth we shall attain to organic liberty—"when each neighbor, yielding to an irresistible law of attraction, will seek a new life in becoming a part of the great whole."

THE RELIGION OF THE FUTURE.

As we grow to organic liberty, legal bandages or restraints will be taken off of the people, and they will have fewer laws and less disobedience. Men will do by nature the things contained in the law. Then will the great heart of humanity grow in our people, until by an all-prevading religious conviction human happiness will be protected as well as human life, and over this great land will grow an empire of mind as well as of might.

With the eyes of Cassandra I see in the far off future and behold the generations of men yet to live under our constitution, governed by an all-prevailing social and religious law of life. On this continent and under our constitution is destined to be developed in the people a new and higher religious sentiment than has yet grown out of the human soul—an all-powerful spirit of good permeating the life-deeds of the people. Such a new manifestation of religion is destined to grow up on this continent. Said Machiavelli, "The greatest man is he who founds a religion for the people, and next to the founder of a religion is he who founds a nation."

The religious idea is the highest idea in man's nature, and it has demonstrated in the Quaker organization, the Mohammedan and Chinese people, a power of unity and use superior to any manifestation of civil government. The operation of these religions in all the activities of life are typical of the new religion of this people, and its principles are now rapidly unfolding on this continent, and will ere long invite the entire people into its simple secrets. The religious sentiment in man is not only the highest, but it has the greatest cohesive power of any element of his mind. It is this pure principle, this unitizing conviction of right and wrong, that is most desired to grow in man until it pervades the national life and unites the entire people with the injunctions of the Higher Law. Its spirit will yet bloom and fraternize the American people as a Magnolian thought of the human soul.

THE PARTY OF THE FUTURE.

To vindicate substantially what I have presented with other matters of national concern, and relating to our civilization, I anticipate at an early day the birth of the party of the future. It will be made of the active, thinking and progressive men of the country. It will announce the essential principles destined to control the political activities of our people during the coming century, and give to this nation a continental life and a proper status before the world.

There is no longer any political party that embodies the vital needs of the people, no party founded upon the principles destined to nationalize this great government and rightly direct its continental growth.

The great men that once gave character and power to the Democratic party now sleep under the sod; they died with the principles upon which that party was founded, and for which they fought its battles before the people and at the ballot-box. The name only remains and serves to represent two antagonistic extremes of political society—opulence and ignorance—two extremes that cannot endure in the progressive march of our humanity. .

So, too, most of the great men that founded and made illustrious the Republican party, have passed from mortal sight into everlasting history and heaven. That party was born of the progressive and religious spirit of the American people. It was organized to achieve an end in the organic condition of the nation; that end has been achieved and a new liberty given to mankind, and a new progress to the nation. But the reactive forces of a constantly growing and progressive national spirit have rendered the Republican party powerless to serve the purposes of the continental life of this great nation. Every succeeding election demonstrates the elements of decay in each party, and the impossibility of either to meet the wants and progressive desires of the American people.

The Presidential campaign of 1876 was nothing but a politicians' squabble for office, and the sequel demonstrated it to be a contest, not of principles but of party names. Neither party declared a single distinctive fundamental principle in its platform, and the people were called upon to vote as the rum-sellers, demagogues and hired politicians directed them. But in vain will the drill-sergeants of decaying party organizations flourish menacingly their truncheons and angrily insist that the files shall be closed and straightened ; in vain will the whippers-in of parties once vital, because rooted in the vital needs of the hour, protest against straying and bolting in the contest of 1880. For that will be one of the most important campaigns ever known to the American people. In it old men and young men will come forth in new political garments, heralding the political faith and practice destined to govern and guide the people and this nation for a century hence.

This new party will be essentially American in its principles and aims, holding that the highest political, industrial and commercial duty of the American people will be to perfect the American government, and give it greater character abroad, and to devote the energies of the American people to the development of the resources of the continent of America and the Western Hemisphere ; and shaping its financial, industrial and commercial policies in harmony with the interests and necessities of our continental people, and especially in accordance with the highest rights and interests of those people living in the Valley of the Mississippi.

That such a new party is now about to be born into existence as a result of a fuller and freer expression of the vigorous and progressive thoughts of the American people, there can be no manner of doubt. Then let us hail such a new manifestation of political life with deeper and more hopeful convictions about the future greatness and grandeur of the American nation, and with renewed energies and higher aims let us go forward with the pure purpose and patriotic devotion of the Roman Cato to contest and to conquer the new and untried problems of the future, remembering that the greatest law-giver is God.

www.ingramcontent.com/pod-product-compliance
Lightning Source LLC
Chambersburg PA
CBHW021429090426
42739CB00009B/1406